HAVE A LITTLE HOPE

AN INSPIRATIONAL GUIDE TO
DISCOVERING WHAT HOPE IS AND HOW
TO HAVE MORE OF IT IN YOUR LIFE

FROM THE AUTHOR OF:

*HOW NOT TO GIVE UP – A MOTIVATIONAL AND
INSPIRATIONAL GUIDE TO GOAL SETTING AND
ACHIEVING YOUR DREAMS*

R.L. Adams

Copyright © 2013 R.L. Adams

All rights reserved.

ISBN-10: 1484865707
ISBN-13: 978- 1484865705

R.L. ADAMS

All Rights Reserved

Copyright © 2013 R.L. Adams. All rights are reserved, including the right to reproduce this book or portions thereof, in any form. You may not distribute this book in any way. No part of this text may be reproduced, transmitted, downloaded, decompiled, reverse engineered, or stored in or introduced into any information storage retrieval system, in any form or by any means, whether electronic or mechanical without the express written permission of the author. The scanning, uploading and distribution of this book via the Internet or via any other means without the permission of the publisher is illegal and punishable by law. Please purchase only authorized electronic editions, and do not participate in or encourage electronic piracy of copyrighted materials.

Legal Notices

The Author was complete as possible in the creation of this book. in this publication, the Author assumes no responsibility for errors, omissions, or contrary interpretation of the subject matter herein. Any perceived slights of specific people or organizations are unintentional.

R.L. ADAMS

CONTENTS

1	11
2	20
3	30
4	52
5	65
6	79
7	96

PROLOGUE

"Hope is the thing with feathers that perches in the soul - and sings the tunes without the words - and never stops at all." — Emily Dickinson

I sit down to write these words about hope after having just watched a powerful and moving documentary on life in North Korea, and I am utterly decimated to the core. When we speak about hope, the general consensus takes a few standards of living into account. We speak about hope from a platform of an already good quality of life afforded to many around the world by their respective governments. But no one can even fathom or come to grips with what it would be like to live in a constant state of fear, famine, and poverty that with which are known in countries where the people live in the shadows of oppressive regimes like in North Korea. For those people, hope takes on an entirely different meaning. When you look at a country like that and you take into account your own woes, things certainly take on a much brighter perspective.

Yet still, we define our present situations through the status quo. We look at what the social norm is in order to judge our current conditions and what we hope for in life. The definition of hope in one country can be far different than it is in another. And for a country like North Korea, hope is buried and mired under the guise of fear; over there, hope is generally sought for the basic necessities in life. People are more concerned with having enough to eat on a daily basis than even being able to conceive of something more grandiose like eating at a fine dining restaurant, let alone having permission to leave the country. In other, better-developed countries, with status quos that call into account a higher standard of living, things are certainly far more different. But hope, no matter where you are, still is where the heart is. Whether you are in the deluge of an oppressive regime like the North Koreans are, or you live in the center of a thriving metropolis with a booming economy, hope will always be where the heart is.

Wherever it is that you live in this world, hope has a certain meaning in your own heart. It takes on a certain form in your mind when the word is uttered, and evokes a certain emotional response. The word hope can be a powerful word that can stir up vivid and graphic images of a desire for a better life, greater health, or a brighter and better future for your children. That same hope is what you harbor in your heart, whether it's a burning desire, or a pilot light that's always on and remains aflame in you always.

Whatever meaning or emotional-shape the word hope takes on for you, the basic assumption of hope is in the expectation of better things to come. It's the belief that things are going to get better no matter what your present situation. We all have the flame of hope lit in our hearts. For some of us, that flame burns brighter and hotter, taking center stage in the desires and pursuits of their lives. For others, the flame of hope stays lit like the burning embers of a once large fire, always simmering somewhere in the background, just waiting to be stoked when the opportunity is right.

However, the problem at hand is how you can take the flame of hope that's lit in your heart, and use it to spark a wildfire of action that will produce the results of your dreams. It's this type of hope that we all seek; it's a solid sense of hope deep-rooted in past experiences – both of your own and that of others – and a true expectance in positive future outcomes. That's the hope that most of us are searching for, but that most of us simply cannot find. But by stirring up that hope, you can locate that final sense of perseverance that it's going to take you to push through your limitations and achieve your dreams. It's there, deep inside of you, just waiting to be let free.

In life, we all struggle and we all face setbacks. But, those failures are what define us; they make us grow and mature, and through those tough times we are able to appreciate the good times. If you've failed at something in your life, and your plans came apart, there's still hope on the other end. Maybe your business has failed, or maybe it's your relationship, or quite possibly your health, but whatever it is, this little book about hope will give you the inspiration and motivation to see yourself through the tough times, whatever that may be for you right now.

Hope has taken on a certain meaning for me today, because of the experiences in my life. Like me, your hope is founded on your beliefs, beliefs that are shaped by your own experiences. But, if you're looking for a little bit of hope and inspiration, and want to expand your beliefs on what is possible in this world, then this little book of hope is just for you. We all need a little bit of extra inspiration and hope in our lives, because most of the time, we can all hit a rut, and face life's lows. And, when we're in our day-to-day lives of just living on autopilot, it's hard to pinpoint the things that matter and make efforts towards fixing them. But this little book of hope will help you do just that.

1
THE MEANING OF HOPE

"My great hope is to laugh as much as I cry; to get my work done and try to love somebody and have the courage to accept the love in return." – Maya Angelou

Have you ever wondered what it is about bad situations that seem to bring out the best in people? If you've ever had something really bad happen to you in your life, then you know what I'm talking about here. It's in those situations that the best in us seems to come out. Has this happened for you? I know it certainly has for me, and it most likely has for you as well. This personal journey that we take in the face of calamity and strife, helps us dive through the sea of emotional turmoil that we all have to swim through in life, to reemerge on the other end as stronger individuals. We're able to find it within ourselves to somehow make it through, and it's part of our survival instinct; we adapt in order to survive.

If you're struggling through a difficult situation right now in your life, and you're trying to hold onto some semblance of hope through it all, then you're not alone. We all face difficult situations in life, and it's those difficult situations in life that tend to define us as human beings. But, the truth is that human beings are not only built to survive, we're built to thrive. If you've studied successful individuals, or read up on how someone came to become successful, no matter what walk of life they are from, you'll notice a major trend about them: they've all failed many times over before succeeding. Whether we're talking about Henry Ford, Walt Disney, Thomas Edison, Stephen King, Stephen Spielberg, or the countless others out there who have achieved major success, they all failed in life many times before they succeeded. But one thing is for certain: they all kept the flame of hope alive no matter how many times they failed.

Life isn't about your failures, or how bad things can seem when you fail; life is about what you do in the face of failure. For some people, survival is merely enough. They take a bad situation, persevere and when they get to the other end, they achieve a complacency and are simply happy enough to be past the strife. For others, survival is not enough. They take that bad situation in their lives, and they use it to propel themselves forward; they thrive. Whatever situation or stage of life you're in right now, if you're struggling, then there is always hope. Hope is something that exists to remind us that, no matter how bad things may be, and no matter what's happened to you in your life, that there are still good things to come. It's a belief in your self that no matter what is going on or how bad the situation may seem, better things are on the horizon.

But we all know that when we're faced with times of struggle, it isn't always that easy to be hopeful. It's very easy to get emotionally sidetracked isn't it? I know that there was a time in my own life, a time that I would almost rather not remember, where hope's beacon faded for me. It was a time when I was faced with so much pain and agony that, although I didn't want to go on, something deep down inside of me pushed me forward; something propped me up. But, although this was a time in my life that failure took center stage, I feel like it was a time in my life that, had I not experienced it, I wouldn't be where I am today.

Emotional rock bottom was a strange concept to me before then. I had never experienced the type of emotional emptiness and complete despair and defeat that happened when my life caved in on itself. I remember sitting on the beach one day sometime afterwards, watching the sunset and realizing what my life had come to and all the people that I had hurt. It was brutal. But out of that really bad situation, came a lot of really good. I went from having a lot of hope, to having no hope at all, to then having more hope than I have ever had. Yes, it was a bit of a rollercoaster ride, and at the time I cursed everything that I could as the source of the problems. I didn't seem to be able to look inwards and be honest with myself, but then everything changed; my entire outlook and look on life, hope, and my dreams shifted.

The dramatic shift that occurred in my life took some deep soul searching and digging. It took a lot of reflection and conversation with others around me to truly look inward at what I was doing wrong. But the problem in life usually is that most of us cannot be honest about how our behaviors are negatively affecting us, and the people around us. Until things get really bad, or you hit an emotional rock bottom, that honesty is as rare as finding a needle in a haystack. It's unfortunate that it usually takes a tragic or drastic occurrence to make us come to certain realizations in life, but that's sometimes just the way it is.

It's funny how things happen that way in life. Out of a really bad situation for me, came a lot of really good. Maybe I'm a big proponent and believer in things happening for a reason, but, as more time fills the space between myself and the drastic events in my life, I realize that those are the things that have defined me; it was out of those situations that I was able to gain my true identity into who I really am. And if you're struggling through something that seems like it's insurmountable right now, take it from me and know that "this too shall pass."

Whatever it is that you're going through right now, whatever the pain or agony you're facing, you will get through it. How quickly you're able to let go and move on is entirely up to you. Sometimes, things are simply out of our control, and you have to learn how to let go and not try to over analyze or entirely control a situation. What will come to pass will come to pass, so take solace in that fact, and in the fact that whatever it is that you're struggling with, millions have faced before you and millions more will face after you.

WHAT IS HOPE?

If you are struggling with something right now in your life, or you have in the past, then you've had your fair share of dealing with hope in your life. Hope exists in so many different forms today, but even in its most minimal form of being something that will simply get you through the next day, we all need hope in our lives to survive. Hope is a necessity for us to go on, because when we lose all hope, that's when life takes a drastic turn for the worse. These are the people that lose that glimmer in their eyes and begin to start imagining all the calamity and strife that they are about to face and begin to imagine a future with no hope at all.

For people with very little hope in their lives, it's not for lack of them not wanting it to exist, but rather it's that these people feel that there is no set of beliefs generated by personal experiences or the experiences of others, for them to build a foundation for hope to exist. And that's a scary thought. If you've ever felt hopeless in your life, maybe you know what I'm talking about. You might not understand hopelessness in the sense that a North Korean might, who has battled the oppression and fear of a communist regime that is starving its people to death and making them constantly fear for their lives. But you might understand it in different terms.

I know that in my own life, I've certainly felt hopeless before. In fact, I've felt completely powerless, as though nothing that I could possibly do, think, or say would change the future outcome of my circumstances. It's a time in my life where I felt the rawest emotions known to mankind; it's that time when something so traumatic happens that you are emotionally leveled to the ground like a building in an earthquake. The pain and agony that these points in your life can cause are dramatic, to say the least. It's as though everything you once hoped for, and everything you once dreamed of comes crashing down in an instant all around you. At that point in my life, I know that I could have used a little bit of hope in my life; and we all can when faced with situations like that.

However, the sad truth is that this loss of hope happens every second of every day countless times over across the globe. You're not alone in this world if you've lost hope because of an experience that has led you to believe that your future outcome will not be better tomorrow than it is today. But why does this happen? How does one go from having so much hope and so much confidence in what the future may bring, to being completely hopeless? How does the belief that things will be better and brighter in the future disappear? This has certainly happened to me, and, if you're reading these words right now, maybe it's also happened to you.

MY PERSONAL JOURNEY

My life was one big emotional rollercoaster ride for quite some time and I didn't really know how to get off. I thought that my way of thinking was the right way, and that I was doing the right things towards the attainment of what I thought I wanted. I had hopes, dreams, and expectations for the future that began to materialize and come to pass. As each dream was realized something happened to me internally; there was some shift. I would achieve something then suddenly be unhappy again, then try to fill that void with something else.

    I knew that those feelings that I felt couldn't be unique to just me. I knew that other people must have been feeling those feelings as well, so I took solace in that. Those feelings of hopelessness and despair are truly some of the worst moments of my life and just the mere thought of being back in that emotional rock bottom scares me. If you're in that place right now, then my heart goes out to you, it truly does. Because, sometimes, even when we do everything in our power to control a situation and make it better, things still come crashing down.

We all go through those emotional rock bottoms. It's just that some people go through them more often than others and feel them more severely than others. Depending on the type of person you are, these may feel like mild tremors that happen every so often, or they may feel like high magnitude earthquakes that shatter your entire world. Whatever type of emotional bottoms you've experienced, if you're looking for some hope and some inspiration in your life to help you out of them, then you truly need to dig deep down inside and be ready to change.

However, not only must you be ready to change, you must be ready to be honest with yourself and actually make a shift in your thinking. Because you have to understand that the things in your life that have happened to you have a reason to them. However much you like it or not, those things will help you in some way or another, at some point or another; it's just hard to see it when you're so close to incidents of pain and failure.

I truly feel that everything in life happens for a reason. Think about your life, and all the things that you do in the day, all the places that you go and the people that you interact with; sometimes, you feel this strange coincidence deep down inside, like something happened to you for a reason. If you've ever felt this then you know exactly what I'm talking about. I guess I say this because writing these words for me happened for a reason, and you reading them right now happened for a reason. You had to do thousands of different things in your life to come to this page and read these words. It happened for a reason.

The notion that things happen for a reason is

important; it's important when it comes to defeating hopelessness and despair in your life. I know that in my life, many things have happened that I once thought had absolutely no reason. I recall cursing everyone aside from myself for the calamity and strife that I suffered in my life. I was fed up and couldn't take it anymore; it felt like everywhere I turned more bad things happened. But then one day that all changed. Some sort of mental and emotional shift occurred that was truly remarkable and dramatic. Everything that I ever was, and everything that I ever thought was important changed in the blink of an eye. All of a sudden I had hope.

2
THE ORIGINS OF HOPE

"You may not always have a comfortable life and you will not always be able to solve all of the world's problems at once but don't ever underestimate the importance you can have because history has shown us that courage can be contagious and hope can take on a life of its own." – Michelle Obama

It was almost like any other day for 8-year old, Michael. His mother woke him up for school, helped him get dressed and poured him a bowl of his favorite cereal of Crunchy O's for breakfast. Except on that day, something different happened. When the phone, rang, Michael's mother stared at it for a moment. It was her husband, and it was most likely the news that she had been expecting.

Several days ago, Michael's little sister, 6-year old Kaylie, had fallen ill and was taken to the hospital. "Is it Kaylie, mommy?" The little boy looked up at his mother as she eyed the caller ID on the cell phone. "Yes, dear it's

Kaylie."

"Honey?" said the voice on the other end of the line.

"Peter? What is it?" her heart fell into her stomach even before her husband could speak.

"Honey, it's bad news. The doctor just left and I'm standing outside of the room but... it's bad news."

"Oh my God," she said. "What is it?"

"Honey, sit down for a minute." she took a seat while Michael sat at the kitchen table with his spoon suspended in mid-air while studying the reaction of his mother on the telephone.

"What is it? Tell me?" she cupped her hand on her mouth, while the little boy looked on wondering what was going on. She couldn't look her son in the eyes.

"It's... it's cancer."

Dead silence on the line as Michael's mother sat motionless.

"Honey? Are you there?"

Silence.

"Yes. Yes... I'm... I'm here. I just can't. Are they... sure?" Michael stopped kicking his feet and stopped eating altogether and looked at his mom. The 8-year-old knew something was wrong.

"What are we going to do? What happens now?" She said the words very, very slowly, as if in a trance. "My little girl..." Tears swelled in her eyes and she started sobbing.

"Mommy?" Kaylie took the phone. "Mommy, it's okay

mommy. Please don't cry."

When she heard her daughter's voice she tried to pull herself together but she had difficulty. "Baby? Baby, it's going to be okay. We are going to find you the best doctors and get you feeling better, okay?" She wiped the tears from her eyes.

"Mommy, they said that Mikey could help me get better. He can fix me."

"Sweetie, put daddy back on the phone for a minute okay? Mommy loves you."

"Love you too, mommy."

"Honey, are you there?"

"Yes," Peter replied.

"What does she mean? Mikey can fix her?"

"Yes, well… they're willing to try a unique surgery, but Michael's is the only exact HLA-match for the bone marrow transplant. It's complicated. It's the Human Leukocyte Antigen and it needs to be a match otherwise the body might attack the transplanted marrow."

"Oh," she said still sitting motionless and wiping tears from her eyes.

"Honey, can you put him on the phone? Can you put Michael on the line?"

"Yes." She handed the phone to her son. "Sweetheart, your daddy wants to speak to you."

"Daddy?" Mikey snatched the phone from his mom.

"Mikey, your sister is sick and she needs your help. It's

a matter of life and death."

"Okay, daddy. I'll do it," said the little boy on the phone.

After the surgery was completed and Michael came to in the recovery room, he looked up to see both his parents smiling down at him.

"Mommy? Daddy? Is Kaylie okay?"

"Yes, sweetheart," said his mother, "she's going to be okay now thanks to you."

The little boy smiled up at them. "Okay that's good. How long do I have left to live?"

"What do you mean?" The boy's father crinkled his face.

"You said it was a matter of life and death, daddy? When will I die?" The little boy looked up curiously.

Both parents looked at one another, and then looked down at their son. They realized that their son thought that if he had the surgery, he would die and his sister would live.

"Honey, you're not going to die, but you did save your sister's life." They smiled warmly at the little boy who seemed confused but happy that his sister would be okay.

*****

Hope can mean so many different things to so many different people. As in this little story depicted of a young boy who saves his sister with an operation that he thought meant he would die, hope can be present in our lives in so many different ways, but it's that same hope that keeps us moving on. And depending on your present situation in life, hope has a unique meaning to you. To some, hope can be something as basic as the desire to get through the next day without pain for people battling terminal diseases like cancer. For others, hope can be a string of goals and desires carefully crafted in their mind that they are working towards and striving for.

However hope looks for you right now, hope, in the true meaning of the word, is the belief that circumstances in your life are going to get better. It's the feeling that no matter what your present situation is like, and no matter how bad or bleak it may seem, that it's going to improve. You may not be quite sure at the moment how it's going to improve, but you believe, deep down inside your heart, that it will. It's this belief that many of us are chasing, because without this belief reasons for going on and continuing in light of a dark situation begin to fade.

Without hope we are truly lost. If you're struggling through a dark and dire situation right now then you need hope in your life. You need a reason to wake up the next day and continue the fight for whatever it is that you're trying to overcome or accomplish. Whether you brought your present situation on yourself, or some external forces were responsible, hope is like the rope thrown from the boat of life that is your lifeline to salvation and inner peace. It's what we're all chasing.

WHERE DOES HOPE COME FROM?

Hope is based on belief, and your belief systems are what make you who you are. In life, we all operate from a modus that works within the confines of those beliefs. For some, whose beliefs are grandiose, most things don't seem that out of reach. However, for others who harbor smaller belief systems, those same things may seem insurmountable. But where do these beliefs stem from? How is that two individuals who can be almost identical in every way, have two such drastically different belief systems?

Beliefs come from a lot of places. They are interlaced in your genetic fiber, which develops through societal and environmental exposure to people and situations. Basically, beliefs are formed from your experiences and your personal analysis of those experiences. Since we are the product of those experiences and each one of us has a unique set of experiences throughout our entire lives, even if we were to experience the same thing as another individual at the same time, our response will be based on beliefs already developed prior to that situation.

When you develop a belief, you subconsciously hold that belief as the truth, and nothing outside of that truth can really exist for you in the confines of your own world. Even if, for example, you know for a fact that something is achievable because someone else has done it somewhere else in the world, to you, that's an anomaly and outside of your belief system. For example, many people have beaten cancer through the power of their beliefs, yet, even though this is the case, people still harbor the belief that once you get cancer, it's all over.

But it's hard to overcome that which we feel is mentally insurmountable at times. Sometimes, our subconscious mind takes over our thoughts and produces beliefs for us even when we aren't paying attention. Because when someone develops the belief system that anything is possible in the world if you just apply yourself, obstacles begin to crumble right before their eyes. There's a lot to say about harboring beliefs like this.

WHAT WE'RE CAPABLE OF

Human beings are capable of doing so much and accomplishing so many things, because we've learned to expand our beliefs. What was impossible only a few years ago, is now possible today. That's because when you learn to widen your beliefs you can sow the seeds of hope for reaping your dreams or overcoming your obstacles in the future.

Without hope, where would we be today? What would the world look like if we didn't have something to hold on to, cherish, or look forward to? Without hope, how would we get past times of war, times of oppression, and times of hatred? Without hope, in those times, we would emotionally perish, because without it there truly ceases a reason to exist.

If you think for a moment about someone in a dire

situation at one point in his life such as Nelson Mandela, the South African leader who was sentenced to life in prison in 1962, and think what would have happened to him without hope? Mandela emerged 27 years later to tackle some of the toughest issues in the South African society and blaze a trail towards apartheid and equality in rights, and eventually became the President of the country. What would have happened if Mandela would have lost all hope in prison?

Hope is a powerful thing and it is exists in us all. Just like the hope in Mandela, hope, and the belief that circumstances will get better, has been a resounding theme in people who have tackled social and political inequality throughout the world. People like Dr. Martin Luther King Jr. who had the hope and the dream that all people, who were created equally, would also be treated equally. Dr. King hoped that one-day all men, women and children would be treated the same no matter the color of their skin, nor the origin of their birth. No matter where you were from, he hoped that each one of us would be treated the same way.

Hope exists and permeates every aspect of our lives, and throughout history through to modern day, stories of hope have evaded our lives. From the hope to improve their grades for students in school, to the hope to improve their financial situations to individuals in the work field, to the hope to improve their health for those struggling with illnesses, hope is everywhere we turn. Without that hope, those same people would struggle to push through, especially when times get very tough. We all need a little bit of hope to hold on to, no matter who we are or what we do, nor what our present situations are in life.

Just like the story of little Michael, out of a really bad situation, came some really good. In the process, the seeds of hope were sowed by the little boy, and then reaped by the entire family. It was a pure blind hope that touched the parents' hearts and showed them what really mattered in life. That situation was one of the most difficult situations that family had ever faced, but it brought them together. Those hopes and dreams for a happy and healthy daughter brought each and every one of them closer to each other. But that's what hope should do. Hope should be the guiding light in a time of darkness; it should be the lighted path in a dark forest. That's what hope is, and that's what hope should always be.

3
ALTERING YOUR BELIEFS

"Beliefs have the power to create and the power to destroy. Human beings have the awesome ability to take any experience of their lives and create a meaning that disempowers them or one that can literally save their lives." – Tony Robbins

Amy Tan, the best selling author of *The Joy Luck Club* knows what it feels like to start with a limiting set of beliefs. As the daughter of Chinese immigrants, Tan, never had any true personal experiences, or the direct experiences of her family members, that she could rely on for success in her family. There was nothing in her life, no situations that proved that she could become successful as an author. She merely relied on her own capabilities and convinced herself that she would succeed doing something that she loved to do.

But Tan first didn't start her writing career as a creative writer. When she sat to write, she did it as a means to generate an income for herself. With a business partner Amy Tan launched a career in technical writing for business professionals. She wrote speeches for sales executives of large corporations. But one day she had a dispute with her business partner who thought she should give up writing to focus on the management side of the business. Amy Tan found herself being distracted by other creative outlets such as jazz piano and eventually ceased doing business with her business partner and struck out as a freelance writer full-time.

So Amy Tan was a woman on a mission. Somehow, she manifested the belief deep down inside of her that she could make it as a best selling author. And she did. But what sets someone like Amy Tan apart from anyone else in the world trying to chase his or her dreams? She developed the belief that she could do it. And having the belief that you can accomplish something is a very powerful tool. With a strong enough belief in yourself, you can move mountains and accomplish just about anything.

*****

Everyone in life has a set of beliefs, and those beliefs are what define us. They allow us to go about our days with certain expectations based on past experiences or the experiences of others that shape the way we think and act. When a situation is foreign to us, we rely on our knowledge in the experience of similar situations or in the experience of others in order to better judge our own expectations. But those same set of beliefs that define us, can also severely limit us. It can force us to become stifled in our inability to act based upon what we think is possible in the world. It can limit us in the sense that it can stop us from really reaching for the stars due to a very low level of expectations set for ourselves.

Your own beliefs right now are what shape your thoughts and are acting as a borderline for the realm of possibility for you. If you've tried something in the past and you failed, then you might attribute the belief of failure to any similar situations in your life. For example, if you launched a business and you failed at it, and you had to shut it down to go back to a 9 to 5 job then you might harbor a negative set of beliefs towards being in business for yourself. Or similarly, if you've tried to go on a diet in the past and in your own eyes you failed, you might attribute negative feelings of pain and failure to dieting. These personal experiences can have a very dramatic impact on how we look at our own potential outcomes in life when engaged in any pursuit.

We are the definition of our beliefs, but those beliefs usually come from our own experiences or the experiences of others. So why is it that, even when we know that something is possible because others in this world have achieved it, do we still harbor negative beliefs that limit us in our lives? Why is it that we allow those beliefs to hold us back from pushing towards our desired goals and dreams? Human beings are interesting in that way. I'm just as guilty of doing this as is the next person, but it doesn't have to be this way.

Many people simply take the easy way out when it comes to creating a foundation for beliefs that will support their dreams. But, without the proper beliefs, you can't develop the hope to achieve your dreams. Your beliefs will define just what is possible in the realm of your own life, so it's important to take a good hard look at just what it is that you believe in during the pursuit of your hopes and your dreams. If your beliefs don't support those hopes and dreams then you'll find severe difficulty in achieving them.

For example, if your hopes are to start your own business one day, you need to take a look at your beliefs surrounding being in business for yourself. The first few things to look at would be just how much you believe in your own ability to run and manage your own company, no matter how big or small it may be. Do you believe that you can setup a business that would add value to people's lives? Do you have supporting experiences that indicate to you that you are intelligent enough to pull it off? Or, do you have some limiting beliefs that may indicate that you are likely to fail or jump ship as soon as the going gets tough?

Your personal experiences, or the experiences of those close to you, with business will have a major impact on how you define your own beliefs. If you have positive experiences, both in your personal life, and those in the lives of those close to you, then you are more likely to have strong belief in your ability to run your own business. If on the other hand, you have poor experiences of being in business for yourself, or you have several close friends or family members that failed in business, your beliefs may take on another shape. Sometimes, we don't even realize that we harbor these beliefs because our minds go into autopilot when milling these types of decisions over. Something that happened years ago in your childhood may play a major role in your beliefs today. Those early experiences can help or hinder your hopes in aspiring to do just about anything.

Identifying your past experiences and becoming more aware of what it is you believe and why is one of the most important steps in expanding your vision. Many of us know that just about anything is possible, but we're still limited on a personal level because we don't have the belief in ourselves to accomplish certain things. When you take a very close look at the experiences that shape those beliefs, you can help to alter those beliefs so that they support you rather than hinder you in the pursuit of your hopes and your dreams.

HOW TO ALTER YOUR BELIEFS

Limiting beliefs, or beliefs that do not support your hopes, dreams, and desires, can be extremely debilitating. If you find yourself harboring limiting beliefs, then you must take the steps necessary in order to alter and replace them with a new set of beliefs that will support your desired future outcome. No matter what it is that you're hoping for, whether it's for better health, a better career, or better relationships with your friends and loved ones, your beliefs are going to be what help you achieve those hopes and dreams.

For example, let's just say that I believe that all people are liars because I had some very bad experiences with people that I once trusted lying to me and abusing my trust. Yet, even though I may harbor that belief, I may also hope to one day have a better relationship with my spouse or a person I do business with. How will that be possible?

HAVE A LITTLE HOPE

How can I possibly hope to improve on a personal or business relationship when my foundational core belief goes entirely against it? If I were to think that all people are liars, my inability to trust my spouse when I'm unsure of where that person was for the evening or whom they were with, would increase immensely. How would I possibly be able to believe a supplier when they told me that the pricing that they were offering me was the lowest that they could possibly go? Can you see how the belief that all people are liars is going to limit my hopes for a better relationship in work or at home?

Whatever it is that you believe, if it's limiting you, you need to take steps in order to alter those beliefs. But altering one's beliefs certainly is not a simple task. It's because our beliefs are developed over the course of our lives, and they are almost ingrained in us. If your life were like a wood plank, then the grains of wood would be like your beliefs. That's because our beliefs are modeled and shaped based upon our experiences. If I've had the experience of being able to lose 50 pounds within a two-month period, then my belief is that, yes, you can shed 50 pounds in 60 days. If I was never able to do that, or I failed at any diet that I tried, then I might not have that belief unless I built up enough supporting experiences around me in order to support the new belief. Similarly, if I knew someone very close to me who was able to achieve that goal, then my belief may quite possibly be altered.

So, how do you go about altering your beliefs to replace them with new non-limiting ones? How do you go from a place of non-belief in yourself, to complete and utter belief? Well, the process is straightforward, but it is not easy by any means. You have to approach this transformation with true honesty to look at yourself and the way you view things in your life. You must also have a deep and sincere willingness to be more open-minded and to change your ways. But since many people are very steeped in their habits and their beliefs, doing this can be difficult. But, if you are committed enough to your hopes and your dreams, then this should be a priority. If you are prepared to alter your beliefs, then the process will take you through 5 separate steps in order to eradiate, then replace, your old beliefs with new ones.

STEP 1 – BE HONEST WITH YOURSELF

The first step in altering your old beliefs and replacing them with new beliefs that will support your hopes and your dreams is to be honest with yourself about your present beliefs. It's easy to overlook certain beliefs that you may harbor as a "given," but nothing is a given that doesn't support your intended future outcome. Again, an example would be if you hope that you could one day buy your own home, you must first identify any beliefs that would be holding you back. For example, your limiting beliefs might be that, you don't have enough saved up as a down payment, or your credit isn't good enough, or your income isn't high enough. Whatever your beliefs are that may be limiting you, identify them and be honest with yourself.

Since these beliefs are based upon personal experiences or the experiences of those close to you, you need to take a very close look at why you feel the way you do. You have to analyze the experiences that brought you to harbor these beliefs in the first place. Maybe you've had trouble paying your rent in the past, or maybe you had a friend who tried to get a loan and got declined because of their certain credit score or the amount of money they had to put down. Just maybe you're basing your beliefs on these types of experiences, which may be limiting your ability to own a home.

If you find yourself harboring these types of limiting beliefs, the first thing that you need to do is congratulate yourself in the first place for spotting them. It's not easy to take a look at yourself in careful analysis and spot what's wrong or what's limiting you based upon your past experiences or the experiences of others. Today, most people need the help of others or feedback from others in order to spot their own shortcomings. If you've come to your own realizations about your beliefs through the feedback from others that's okay as well, but your true inward and honest look at yourself is what's going to allow you to progress beyond your limiting beliefs. The goal is to remove these limiting beliefs and replace them with new beliefs that will support your hopes and dreams.

When you can be truly honest with yourself, and recognize that your beliefs that you have been harboring have not been serving you and you're ready to make a change, you can begin the process of getting on the road to true hope again. Take a look at your current beliefs from an honest perspective and see which ones have not been serving you, and mentally prepare yourself for a major shift in your thinking.

STEP 2 – MAKE A DECISION TO CHANGE

Once you can be honest enough with yourself to be able to identify the beliefs that may be limiting you in your life, you then need to make a decision to change. This decision is critical because if you back this decision with enough emotional fuel, then changing your beliefs will come much easier for you. If you are unable to attach the required emotional fuel to your decision to replace your limiting beliefs with new supporting ones, then your chances of success will greatly diminish.

For example, extending on the example of owning your own home, let's just say you have identified the experiences that are shaping your limiting beliefs today. Your next step would be to make a decision to change, but that decision to change has to be emotionally charged. What is it about those limiting beliefs that have been hurting you? Think about it for a moment.

Attach enough emotional fuel to no longer wanting to be imprisoned by your old beliefs. Maybe you hate those beliefs now because if you continue to harbor them you'll never be able to provide a proper family home for your children in the future. Or maybe, if you continue harboring those beliefs you'll suffer a major financial blow and set back in life, unable to progress by not being able to own your own home. You need to associate enough emotional hatred to not owning your own home in order to supersede the old limiting beliefs.

Remember that human beings do more to avoid pain than they will to gain pleasure. For example, by April 15th in the United States, most people will do whatever it takes to get their taxes done by the deadline, even if it means doing them all night long in the hours leading up to the due date. This is because they know that not getting it done will be far more painful than turning them in on time. Up until that point the pain doesn't exceed the pleasure of not getting it done. This is also why students cram for exams and papers that they haven't studied for; they realize that it will be far worse for them not to turn it in than if they do. So try to associate as much pain to the old behavior in order to step away from it.

When you make a decision to change your limiting beliefs, you make a commitment. Commitments are important in life and we all make them, but making a sincere commitment to change is not simple. You need to find a way to stoke the emotional fuel for change by truly looking at just how your limiting beliefs have been holding you back in life. Maybe your limiting beliefs have held you back from striking out on your own in finding a new job, starting your own business, buying that new home, losing weight, or any number of other things. You need to attribute enough pain to the limiting behaviors of your past in order to make that mental shift in your present behaviors and beliefs in order to achieve the hopes and dreams of your future. Without these new beliefs, you will be stuck back in your old routines wondering why things never seem to get better in your life.

STEP 3 – REPLACE YOUR LIMITING BELIEF

Once you have identified your limiting beliefs and you've made a decision to change, the next step is to begin replacing your limiting beliefs with new ones. For example, let's say you're a student with the hope of becoming an investment banker some day, but you may have some limiting beliefs tied to this hope. Here are some example limiting beliefs that may hold you back from pursuing a career as an investment banker:

- I'm no good in math, because I do poorly on my math tests.

- I don't know how to manage my own money since I have a lot of debt.

- I'm really bad at saving and investing my money.

As you can see, these types of limiting beliefs can keep you in a state of inaction due to the fear that your existing beliefs will not support your desired hope and outcome. Someone who harbors these beliefs is unlikely to pursue a career in investment banking, even if they have a distant feeling that one day they hope to become one. In order to replace these limiting beliefs, you need to first come up with some reasons or excuses for the limiting beliefs.

For example, if your first limiting belief is that you're no good in math because you do poorly on your math tests, then find out why it is that you do poorly. Maybe you do poorly because you don't study enough, or you're too distracted with other things that have been going on in your life. Maybe you do poorly in math because you aren't in class enough to absorb the material, or you don't read through the assignments and complete them in full when they are given. You could say, *"Yes, I've done poorly on my math tests, but that's only because I haven't really applied myself lately. From here on out I am going to do all the assignments in full, attend every class, and apply myself more."*

In the other examples, again, find excuses for your past beliefs. If you said that you don't know how to manage money because you have lots of debt, take a look at why you really have lots of debt. Maybe you have lots of debt because you've been spending carelessly on things, or you have a lot of debt because you have a lot of monthly payments that you've had for a long time as a result of some poor decisions that you made in the past. Maybe you have a lot of debt because you go out to eat too often, or you like to take vacations every month. Your new beliefs may say something like, *"Yes, I've made some bad decisions and accumulated a lot of debt in the past, but moving forward I plan to tackle this problem head on, crunch the numbers and create a budget that I will stick to."*

Whatever it is that you find is limiting you, destroy those limiting beliefs by coming up with some honest excuses as to why you believe the way you do in order to set the foundation for altering those beliefs. Once you do this, simply replace your old beliefs with new ones. For example, in the first limiting belief, we could say that, *"I am excellent at math when I apply myself. In fact, I can excel at anything when I apply myself."* Can you see how this new belief will support your hope of becoming an investment banker?

STEP 4 – FIND YOUR INSPIRATION

No matter what it is in life that you hope for, or that you struggle with, you can achieve it or overcome it by altering your belief system. One excellent way to solidify your new beliefs into place is to find inspiration in others. There is a lot to say for looking at others' past experiences in order to develop your own beliefs. Some people refuse to do this, and seem to isolate those experiences as abnormalities that most people are incapable of. Taking this approach is wrong. Instead, you need to take an approach that uses other peoples' past experiences as inspiration for the new belief that you can do it too.

For example, if you have a certain hope such as owning your own business some day, and you don't have the personal experiences to back up beliefs that would support this hope, then look outwards. You can do this by looking at others that were in similar situations as yourself that were able to start their own businesses. Look to those that started businesses similar to the one that you're interested in starting and model yourself after them. Look to their experiences and see just what it is that they did to get off the ground, in order to try and find your own sense of inspiration. Many people have struggled and persevered through far more difficult times than you have to achieve their hopes and their dreams.

In today's society, it's difficult not to be inspired by what others have achieved, especially the so-called "new rich," who are glorified by the media. The problem is that, most people look at the "haves" but don't realize what they did to get to where they are. They don't see the years of blood, sweat, and tears that they poured into their respective fields of work in order to master their trade or skill. They don't look at all of the setbacks that they faced and the struggles they had to overcome. It's easy to overlook these details because they're not publicized for the most part. The media is only concerned with glorifying the rich lifestyles that some of these people lead, but if you take a good look at their past, you'll see the struggles that they persevered through.

Did you know that Colonel Sanders, the founder of Kentucky Fried Chicken, failed most of his life? Did you also know that it wasn't until the age of 65 years old, and with a social security check for $105 in his pocket, that he drove around to every single restaurant he could find in order to pitch them his chicken recipe. 1009 different restaurants rejected him and said no before he found someone willing to take a chance on him. Yes, he failed 1009 times before he succeeded. Most people thought he was a crazy old man in a white suit with some chicken recipe, yet no one realized just what this man had: a burning hope and desire that was unparalleled. How many people do you think could stand rejection over 1000 times before succeeding? How many people do you think told Colonel Sanders he was nuts and that he should quit? One could only imagine the very strong belief systems he had to have in order to support his hopes. He knew, without a shadow of a doubt, that he would succeed. He didn't know how, but he just knew that he would.

Did you know that The Beatles were rejected countless times before a label signed them? One label went as far as saying that "guitar groups are on the way out," and "the Beatles have no future in show business." However, that same group that "had no future in show business," went on to sell 2 billion records. 2 billion. Thomas Edison failed over 10,000 times to try to invent electricity. Stephen King was rejected 41 times by publishers, and has since sold over 350 million books. John Grisham was rejected 28 times but has gone onto sell more than 250 million books. People like Stephen Spielberg, Vincent Van Gogh, Dr. Seuss, Mark Cuban, and many others all failed before they succeeded, but somehow they were able to instill a belief system in themselves so strong, that nothing could stop them, not even 10,000 failures.

Search the Internet, or ask a friend to find examples of others who have succeeded where you have failed. Find people in similar situations, or with similar stories that have accomplished what you hope to in your life. No matter what your hope is, someone else has done something similar. Seek them out, find them, and study them. What does it take to be like them and to have their beliefs and desires? How can you instill a little bit of what they had into your own life? Once you find someone similar, read his or her story. Take a look at what it is they did, or had to struggle through in order to achieve their hopes and their dreams. No matter what this is, modeling your beliefs based on those who have succeeded before you is a very powerful tool in success thinking. No matter what it is, even if you're battling a terminal illness or some other major calamity such as a court case, a death of a loved one, and anything else, look to others who have struggled through the same to persevere.

STEP 5 – TAKE MASSIVE ACTION

Never leave the site of setting a goal or envisioning a hope without taking massive action. It's important that you take the steps that I've laid out here without walking away from this. Because, if you take a little bit of action every single day, and you string those days together, you will be amazed at your progress over an extended period of time. Don't get discouraged if you don't see results overnight. Rome wasn't built in a day. But when you stick it out and persevere, that's when the real magic happens. It happens by taking daily and consistent action over and over again.

When you're working on something major like altering your beliefs, you truly have to achieve some new emotional connectedness to your new replacement beliefs. If you can't emotionally connect with them strongly enough, then your old beliefs will find their ways right back into your life and begin diminishing your hopes and your dreams. Don't let that happen. Emotionally connect to the change then take massive action towards changing.

To get started, grab yourself a piece of paper and separate it into three columns. In the first column, write out what your hopes and your desires may be, in the second column write out what your present beliefs are that affect each hope, and in the third column, write out the new beliefs that would have to replace your old ones in order to be able to support your hope. If you're serious about creating more hope in your life, then you have to physically do this exercise. Don't pass it up and continue reading on. Take action and actually grab a pen and paper and do the exercise. There's something visceral that takes place when you physically involve yourself in these types of exercises. If you haven't been getting the results that you've wanted in the past, it could be because you haven't actually applied yourself; you haven't actually taken enough action.

Beliefs can also be ingrained into your subconscious through your family or close relationships. When you were younger, if you heard certain statements uttered over and over again such as "money doesn't grow on trees," "money can't buy happiness," or "champagne tastes and a beer budget," they are not going to support you if your hope is to own a home in the next year or make a million dollars. Although some of these statements are clichés heard throughout societies, they can also eat away at your beliefs when they run contrary to them. You have to replace these limiting beliefs with new ones and find strong enough support for the new beliefs.

Once you have your new beliefs in place to support your hopes, you have to create a game plan for yourself. You need to lay out just how you plan to reach your goals, your hopes, and your desires. If you hope to own your own home in the next year, what steps do you need to take to make this a reality? What new beliefs do you have to put into place? Once you have those figured out, what actions should you take, right now to make your hope a reality? Well, firstly you should contact a mortgage broker, or several, and setup meetings to discuss your present situation. When you actually pursue your dreams in this way, and you take steps to making it a reality, you experience a major emotional shift.

Each and every day, take action and work on replacing your old limiting beliefs with new ones that will support your hopes. Each and every day take steps on making your hopes a reality by taking a little bit of action. Don't allow yourself to lose the momentum that comes with inaction. Commit to the fact that you will not settle for less anymore and you are going to do what it takes to succeed in the pursuit of your hopes, your dreams, and your desires.

4
HOPE VERSUS OPTIMISM

"Optimism is the faith that leads to achievement. Nothing can be done without hope and confidence." – Helen Keller

Nearly five years ago, Jonathan's life took a turn for the worse when the 47-year-old financial services executive made a tragic error in judgment. One evening, after leaving a party for a coworker at a local bar, Jonathan made the decision to drive home after having one too many drinks. He thought he would be okay since his house was but minutes from the venue, but he was sorely mistaken. After misjudging the distance from the traffic light, Jonathan gunned his SUV to try and cross the intersection in time to make the yellow light, which had turned red far before he reached the intersection. Jonathan plowed into a small compact car just as he crossed into the oncoming traffic.

Jonathan still remembered it like it was yesterday. He could still see the faces of disbelief lit up by the bright lights of his SUV as it smashed and crumpled the car, sending it careening into a light pole and ending in a hunk of twisted metal and carnage. The next couple of days spent behind bars over the weekend for Jonathan was a sobering experience, and he vowed from that point on to get his act together. But, the months that ensued for the middle-aged executive were some of the worst months of his life as he wound his way through the justice system.

Somehow, Jonathan managed to get acquitted of the manslaughter charges that were brought against him, but it was only at the expense of mortgaging his house to the hilt and draining his savings. Shortly thereafter, he was fired from his job, and told he would never be able to work again in the industry. After his girlfriend left him, he threw his hands up in the air in silent resignation; he had had it. A few months passed by and Jonathan eventually lost every last dime he had ever made. Unemployed, when the bank came knocking to take his home he was left with only the clothes on his back and nothing more

In spite of all the setbacks, Jonathan still searched for a job, trying to get his life back together, but he had lost everything and everyone close to him. His reckless disregard for the lives of others cost him so much more than just his financial well-being; he was truly left with nothing. After many months of searching for a new job, Jonathan couldn't land anything that would pay a decent wage. Without a home and the bad credit that proceeded from his trials and tribulations, no employer was willing to stick their neck out for him. Jonathan finally lost it all and slipped into the grips of drug addiction, and as the months wore on, he began to lose his desire to live. He could find absolutely nothing about life worth living.

On one warm sunny day, sitting on a grassy slope adjacent to the underneath of a bridge he had called home at the time, the now homeless Jonathan shot up a vile of potent heroine with his friend, Alex. Jonathan was able to find his misery loves company companion in Alex, a fellow homeless man that lived under the same bridge as Jonathan in the outskirts of Cincinnati, Ohio. But on that day Alex decided to shoot up much more than usual, and ended up overdosing. As the months of drug usage wore on, the two continued to try to chase the high, but were always told never to inject too much for risk of overdosing. Jonathan heeded the warning, but Alex didn't seem to.

Jonathan sat and watched helpless and powerless as his friend convulsed and shook violently on the grass; there wasn't a soul in sight who cared to come help. It was at that point in time when he saw his life flash before his eyes, did he finally realize the direness of the situation he had put himself in. With hope of ever climbing out of the hole he had dug for himself fading, Jonathan wondered where things went wrong. The 45 seconds spent sitting on the grass staring at his friend convulsing and shaking violently didn't seem real to him. He was high and his mind was reeling and he couldn't get himself to focus. Maybe if he had, his friend would still be alive today.

*****

I first heard Jonathan's story one day when he had come in to give a speech at a seminar I had attended a few years back, and I recall being so moved by his story. The man who stood up at the podium that day seemed like a man well beyond his years; he seemed like a broken man who had somehow regained his way. There was this strength about him that was powerful; it wasn't just his story, it was his mannerisms and his spirit.

When Jonathan spoke that day in front of nearly a

thousand people, the audience was moved to tears. As he recounted his story I recall thinking about how someone can go from such high highs to such low lows and I connected with him. But Jonathan's story didn't end there. Sure, he had gone from a financial services executive who owned his own home, to a homeless junky living under a bridge, but somehow he turned it all around again. I wondered to myself, what happened that changed everything. Where did the hope come from? Was it even hope or was it something else.

I think this whole question falls back onto us as humans. Yes, in life when really bad things happen, we tend to do really good. But, this isn't always the case. So what separates situations from one another? How is it that for one person, something really bad can bring out the best, while for others, something really bad can bring out the worst? I think that the answer really boils down to honesty. When you can be honest with yourself, about yourself, and what's going on in your life, it makes a significant difference.

However, the problem is that it's difficult to be honest with your self. No one wants to consider their own actions as being wrong or hurtful to others because we are driven by our egos not to think so. However, when you can look inward and be honest with yourself that your actions have negatively impacted your life, and you can identify the behaviors that have led to those negative results and change them, any one of us can make major strides towards improvement.

R.L. ADAMS

HAVING OPTIMISM

For Jonathan, the entire series of events in his life didn't force him to look inward at himself for a long time. Within the span of one year, he went from an executive position and owning a home, to unemployed, penniless and drug addicted, living under a bridge. It wasn't until he saw death knocking at his doorstep was he able to jar himself out of his situation. Throughout the entire time that Jonathan experienced his difficulties he couldn't be optimistic because there was nothing to be optimistic about. But hope and optimism are two different things to have.

On the one hand, optimism will take a look at the current existing evidence and base the outlook on that. If the evidence looks very good, then optimism is more likely, but if the evidence doesn't look as good, then optimism is unlikely. In Jonathan's situation, there was nothing to be optimistic about. Through some bad choices, his life spiraled downward into the drain in a series of events that all pushed him further and further towards the edge. Eventually, Jonathan was left with nothing, and for him, there was no way to look at the events of his life as being optimistic.

In contrast to optimism, hope is not as steeped in the evidence. Hope can take evidence that may not be all that rosy, like in Jonathan's case, and still construe it as a hopeful situation. Why? Because that's what hope is. Even if you don't have evidence, or there is little evidence to support your hopes, hope still exists. For Jonathan, there was very little hope in his life, but as he explained during his speech, he always had some semblance of hope deep down inside, he just didn't really know how to tap into it.

During a question and answer session with Jonathan, the audience asked him a lot of different questions about his life, and they all wanted to know more about this man who seemed to now have it all together after suffering through such calamity and strife. It turns out that Jonathan didn't have any family at all. His parents died at an early age in a car wreck and his grandmother, who passed away many years before Jonathan even began his career in financial services, raised him. Looking at the evidence, even from a young age, Jonathan didn't have much to be optimistic about, but he had a lot to be hopeful for if he had just stopped and looked.

It's great to be an optimist, but for some people, they simply can't travel down that road. Some people become steeped in the evidence of their lives and begin to focus on all the negative experiences. When this happens, it quite easy to become a pessimist; it's quite easy to give up. But hope is a different animal than optimism. Hope can take evidence from anywhere in the world and construe it as evidence that can work on your behalf. When you have hope, you pull from the infinite resources of the universe that allow you to expand your beliefs beyond just your present situation. Somehow, when seemingly every avenue of hope had vanished for Jonathan, he pulled it from somewhere. Somehow, he reached deep down inside and found the inspiration he needed.

HOPE REVOLUTIONS

Hope is much more of a deep-seated belief in good things to come, and doesn't rely on direct evidence. While personal evidence or experience can help to bolster hope, it isn't necessary for hope to exist. Optimism, on the other hand, is very reliant upon the evidence and it's based on those extrinsic events whereas hope comes much more from within; hope is intrinsic.

Even in light of bad situations, one can have hope, and one can have a lot of it. However, hope can also diminish over time and can be used up like the fuel in an automobile if it's not consistently regenerated. Unlike cars however, the universe has an infinite amount of hope to be tapped into, should you choose to do so. But, we all know that the difficulty with hope is really learning how to tap into that infinite resource that exists for all of us.

When Jonathan lost it all and was left with no house, no money, no friends, and was a slave to addiction, one would have thought that he gave up all hope. But during that question and answer session, Jonathan revealed a lot about what most people tend to go through; he went through a hope revolution. Many people experience hope revolutions, and it seems to come on its own at times without even being beckoned. It comes to us when we are at our darkest hour and it helps to mold and shape us into better human beings.

For the most part, hope revolutions don't happen immediately. Usually, it takes a person many times of making the same mistakes over and over again before they can experience a hope revolution. But that's because people usually aren't ready to tap into the infinite hope that exists in the universe until they can be completely honest with themselves. That honesty usually comes when you are at your darkest hour and you've made those same mistakes over and over again and you're truly ready for a change in your life.

If you could think about hope for a moment being like snow sitting atop of a mountain, and as more time passes by, more snow accumulates. When you experience a hope revolution, it's akin to an avalanche coming down the mountainside. It starts slow but quickly picks up speed as large chunks begin giving way and pushing hope with a mighty force into your life. But that avalanche can be hard to trigger at times, because without some of those triggers going off, people merely stay complacent and don't want to upset their internal status quo.

Today, Jonathan is back in the financial services industry. He's no longer an executive; he's now Senior Vice President of the largest firm in the country. It took him years to regain it all and more, but he is a stronger person now than he ever was. But, as you saw with Jonathan's story, hope diminished for him for quite some time. He had absolutely no reason to go on in life and if things kept going the way they did, he could have been the one that overdosed and died. But he didn't. The trigger of Jonathan's friend dying in front of his eyes, doing the one thing that he had begun doing with a vengeance, self-medicating, was a very sobering experience. It lead Jonathan into rehab, treatment, and back on the road to recovery. But it was an incredible story to hear.

If you've ever heard the story of Soichiro Honda, then you know what hope truly is. Soichiro Honda was the man that founded the now very well known Honda Car Company. But Soichiro Honda didn't have a foundation or evidence for hope in his life. During a time when there was a great depression happening in the United States, the Japanese born engineer, Honda, was determined to perfect the piston ring for an automobile engine. Honda toiled day and night until one day after much work and design he felt like he had succeeded. He took the piston ring to Toyota, which was a very large corporation at the time, with the intent to sell it to them. The engineers at Toyota laughed at Honda and told that the piston rings didn't meet their standards.

After two long years of work on perfecting his piston rings, he finally got Toyota to purchase them under contract, and things were underway. However, in 1941, when Japan entered into WWII, the military took control of his factory, and then in 1942 Toyota took a 40% equity and most of the male employees left. However, Honda didn't give up and he worked day and night, but the factory was bombed and leveled in the war. But Honda didn't give up there either, he then rebuilt his factory only to have it destroyed and leveled by an earthquake in 1945. Could you imagine what this did to the man? Can you imagine how he persevered and remained hopeful through all of this?

Of course we all know the end to the Honda story. Today, Honda is a global corporation with an enormous asset sheet and operations in several countries. The Honda car and motorcycles are some of the best selling in the world, but it was all because one man kept his hope alive and he never gave up. He wasn't an optimist, he was a *hoptimist,* as I like to call it. He kept his hope alive no matter what happened to him. Through all the grief and the strife that he faced, he was still committed. In the face of all of that grief, most people would give up and lose all hope. It's not to say that Soichiro Honda never toiled in despair, but he used that to fuel him to succeed. Can you imagine how much better success tasted for him after struggling through all of those setbacks?

Anytime you experience difficulties in life, and you reemerge on the other end you go through that hope revolution just like Soichiro Honda did, and unless you've been to the dark side and back, it's difficult to truly appreciate just what a hope revolution can do for you. If you've been going through a difficult period in your life, then a hope revolution may be what you need in order to push through and make it to the other end as a stronger, better person. But hope revolutions don't have to be triggered by an event. When you can associate so much pain to your actions in the course and direction of your present life, and you can be honest enough to make decisions to change for the better, you can experience a hope revolution without falling so hard on the ground.

However, it's difficult for most to go through this without the aid of a trigger. It's difficult to open your eyes and see even though things are right in front of you. It's difficult to tune your ears to really listen, even if you've been hearing things over and over for quite some time now. Sometimes, that trigger of a very traumatic experience in your life recalibrates your senses and it allows you to truly listen, and truly see what's going on around you. It's during those times in our lives when we're most vulnerable and honest with ourselves. Our egos diminish into something infinitesimal, and it's at that time we need to pounce on our lives to make the changes we've been waiting to make for a long time coming.

If you've experienced an emotional rock bottom recently or a trigger has gone off in your life that has allowed you to look at things in a new light, and hear things differently, be thankful not hurtful. Yes, it's very difficult to see past the pain, especially when we are in the midst of it, but hold on to your hopes and dreams because big things are on the horizon for you. These events in our lives happen for a reason; it's the time when we need to stop behaving in the way we were behaving and start making the right decisions. What are the right decisions to make? Well, only you know that deep down inside and no one can truly tell you aside from yourself because it's you that needs to be honest enough to make the change.

For Jonathan, it not only took a trigger for him to experience his own hope revolution, it took a trigger at a certain time. As he explained in his speech, the first event that resulted in the casualty of one of the passengers in the vehicle he struck jarred him, but it wasn't enough. After the accident, Jonathan continued to drink and it only snowballed, as the other events in his life got worse. Had he stopped drinking at that point in his life, as he explained, he may have been able to piece his life back together before he went completely broke and homeless. But, Jonathan refused to look inward and be honest with himself at that point in time. It took the trigger of the death of his friend until he was able to be truly honest with himself.

As he explained, that trigger, of his friend dying was so powerful because he related himself to that person so much. Alex was like Jonathan in that they both were coping with similar situations in their lives. They both had good lives until they were gripped by addiction, and they both came into homelessness and drug use only after loosing everything else in their lives. Jonathan realized that the death of his friend could have easily been his own death, and he came to grips with the fact that he wanted to live; he didn't want to die. That one profound experience, Jonathan explained, saved his life. It was ironic that it took the death of his friend to save his own life, but for Jonathan, that's what it took.

We are all faced with difficult periods in our lives. Like Jonathan, many of us struggle through different points in our lives. Unfortunately, all too often many simply give up hope and abandon their desires to fulfill their dreams. It's easy to allow life to get to you in this way, but you have to push against the grain sometimes. You have to look inwards and take a deep look at your life and be honest with yourself. Where did hope go in your life? It's not easy to find when you've lost it, but if you're able to be completely honest and prepared to make some huge sacrifices in life, hope can be found.

5
MOVING BEYOND THE PAST

"Learn from the past, set vivid, detailed goals for the future, and live in the only moment of time over which you have any control: now." – Denis Waitley

Emily sat at her cubicle at work and stared at her computer monitor while her fingers stayed suspended in mid-air. She couldn't think of anything else other than her husband, let alone get any work done. There were dozens of insurance claims that needed to be transcribed before the day ended but her mind was nowhere to be found. Last week, Emily walked in on her husband sleeping with another woman. She left work early that day because she was coming on with the flu, but wasn't expecting what welcomed her at home.

For a long time, Emily had a feeling that her husband was cheating on her, but she was never really able to put her finger on it. With two children together, she didn't want to stir the spot, so they just kept on keeping on like nothing was ever gong on. Maybe Emily went home early that day because she wanted to find what she did, and maybe it was just a coincidence. The thoughts kept racing through her mind as she milled the various possibilities. What was going to happen now?

Emily and her husband had been together for nearly 8 years. They had a tough start to their relationship and it was on and off for a while, but when they finally settled down together and decided to get married, she thought he was the one she wanted to spend the rest of her life with. 8 years, two children, a home mortgage, and a mountain of debt later, she questioned every single decision she had ever made. As she sat there with her fingers suspended in mid-air, unable to type, she thought back to all of the decisions that had lead her up to that point in her life.

Emily called the last week, her week from hell, because everything that could possibly go wrong did. Not only did she catch her husband cheating, she also found out that he had gambled away part of their life savings during the "work trips" he took to Atlantic City every few weeks. Emily's husband was a salesman for a large telecom company and he would always be on the road, traveling to different locations along the Eastern Seaboard, pitching telecom packages to the various corporate clients his company was targeting. Emily felt so stupid.

There was a certain cynicism that crept up into Emily's life after that day. It's almost as if everything that had happened lead her to that one point in her life; it was at that point that she let go. She told herself she would no longer care anymore about the actions of other people, but after the anger wore off, she slipped into a depression. Emily cut off her friends, stopped returning personal emails, and slipped into a cold dark and lonely place. If it wasn't for her kids, she would probably have spent all of her free time locked in a room alone.

Emily felt like she had lost all hope, and that the wrecking ball of her husband's actions demolished all of the dreams and hopes that she had for her future, and the future of their family together. He begged for her forgiveness, but she was done. She kicked him out and threw all of his clothes on the front lawn as a public display of humiliation. The anger and the resentment filled the voids in her heart. Who had she become? She didn't know how she could forgive him for blatantly abusing her trust.

*****

Like Emily, we are all forced to go through situations in life that we're not too fond of. Whether we have to face some sort of public humiliation, personal defeat, financial ruin, or something else, we all tend to look for someone to blame for our woes. We never really look inward, but that's our ego's way of protecting us from the outside world. The ego kicks into autopilot and goes into survival mode. This is because it's difficult to blame yourself when things go wrong in your own life. We look to exterior forces for the blame because blaming ourselves usually means being honest with ourselves for our own behavior, which is rare. And it's difficult to be honest with your self and look at your own actions and behaviors from an impartial point of view.

However, you can't set yourself up for the future, and expect to achieve your hopes and dreams, without letting go of the past. Bad things happen to people all the time, and no matter who you are, what you do or where you live, bad things are bound to happen. But, what's more important is how you deal with the bad situations when they occur in your life. If you can't let go and move past the pain, then you'll be stuck and mired by it for the rest of your life. Although this is easier said than done, recognizing your regrets, anger and hatred is the first step in the healing process for blazing a new trail for hope.

When J.K. Rowling, the British writer responsible for the Harry Potter Series, suffered setback after setback in her life, she never gave up hope of her dreams. She first conceived the idea for the first book in the Harry Potter series in 1990 while on a delayed train traveling from Manchester to London, but didn't actually publish that book for 7 years from that point in time. Rowling had no personal experiences to base her hope off of, and she certainly wasn't optimistic about what was happening in her life. Not only was she living on government welfare at the time, but she also suffered through the pain and anguish of the loss of her mother, and the emotional turmoil of a divorce.

Rowling never gave up hope, however, and through the years she pressed on and kept the hope aflame in her heart. Even dealing with life in complete poverty, J.K. Rowling was able to find the hope and the inspiration buried deep down inside of her to make her dreams come true. She focused instead on her daughter and being able to provide a better life for her in the future. She discarded her personal experiences of despair and defeat and pressed through, looking at inspiration in others. Even though it took her 7 years to go from concept to physical book, JK Rowling persevered and is now one of the wealthiest people in the UK.

Had Rowling lived in the past and not been able to move on from the setbacks that she suffered in life, she would have never been able to find the hope and the inspiration to make her dreams come true. You see, when you dwell in the past, you live a life that consumes your mental, physical and emotional energies retelling or replaying events in your mind. When this becomes your focus, and it consumes you the way these events have a tendency to do, your inability to focus and allow your creative juices to flow, along with your hopes and dreams for the future, increases dramatically.

R.L. ADAMS

ACCEPTING YOUR PAST

Long ago, there were two monks who had gone to take a pilgrimage together, crossing treacherous terrain as they left their monastery for an annual retreat of prayer at a remote location with fellow monks from across the entire region. During this pilgrimage, the monks came across a woman who was weeping by the river. The woman was frightened to cross the river, for she could not swim and feared drowning. When the woman saw the two monks she begged them to help her cross, weeping more and more.

The two monks paused and listened to her request. The younger monk took one look at the woman, scoffed and walked away, as it was forbidden for the monks to touch a woman. The older monk paused for a moment, thought about the decision, and suddenly picked up the woman and aided her across the river. The woman was delighted and went on her way, thanking the monk profusely for his help. This infuriated the younger monk who scolded and chided the older monk as they continued their pilgrimage of prayer. Finally, the older monk stopped, looked at the younger monk and said "I merely carried her across the river, but you have been carrying her this entire time."

Like the older monk who let go of his past, it's important to not allow your past to haunt you and torment you; you have to learn to accept it. Accept the fact that this is your history, and it's very much a part of you. You cannot go back in time and change it, and it does not define you. All too often, people take their past and allow it to define them, and although your past is a part of you, you are not the definition of it. Learn to use your past experiences of upset, pain, and anguish as a roadmap that will help to guide you in the future and make better decisions, rather than allowing it to hold you back from moving forward towards your hopes and your dreams in life.

UNDERSTANDING YOUR PAST

A few years had passed since Emily's troubles had started, which led to her divorce and a complete uprooting of her life, and she came to some important realizations about her behavior as a result of the entire process. With the help of a therapist she was able to identify and understand the impact her own actions had on her relationship. Unable to avoid the pain and the anguish that a situation like that brings on, Emily was forced to cope with her feelings and understand her body's own emotional responses to certain events. A nasty divorce will do that to you.

Emily was angry that her husband cheated on her, and angry that he had uprooted the lives of their children. In fact, she became angry at just about anything her ex-husband did, and took his every action and interpreted them as an intent to maliciously hurt her. She had difficulty taking an honest inward look at herself and her own actions, rather than the actions of others. She was so focused on the anger that she was unable to see anything else.

During Emily's lengthy therapy sessions, which took place for more than a year after her divorce, she came to certain realizations. She had begun the pattern of people pleasing at a very early age. Since she grew up in a very chaotic household, she became a pacifier of people from an early age. Whether it was at home with her parents, or in her relationships, Emily never wanted to rock the boat. She associated conflict with pain, so she did all she could to avoid the conflict, but this is precisely what had made her the way that she was. Her inability to understand how to deal with confrontations, lead her to take on a very passive aggressive role in her relationships. She never tackled the problem head on, but rather chose to ignore it in the hopes that it would go away, getting only angry in private but never making a public appeal of her true feelings to him or anyone else.

Emily's therapist helped her to understand her behaviors of the past, learn to accept what had happened to her, and move on. But, this type of understanding can be done without the aid of a therapist if you can learn to understand that our past behaviors and experiences subconsciously influence our present decisions and actions. Emily was able to trace back, with the help of her therapist, the experiences that lead to her present behaviors.

This identification of past relatable experiences through Reverse Pattern Recognition is important in understanding your present behavior. She had to physically sit down, and trace out all of the times that she behaved in ways that were pacifying in her past relationships. When you identify your past behaviors, your ego can no longer hide from itself, and you can begin the road to understanding, healing, and moving on. But it doesn't require expensive therapy to do this, just an honest approach of looking at your life from a third person's point of view.

LETTING GO OF THE PAST

If you're still holding onto mistakes that you've made in the past, or people that you hurt or those that have hurt you, you have to make a conscious effort to let these go in order to start the healing process and begin a new journey of hope. Whatever it is that you used to hope for, never think that it's a thing long gone and out of the question. If you once hoped for something with so much intent, don't give up on that hope at the mere sight of some resistance. If you failed at something, either move on or keep trying; do it over and over again if you're trying to succeed at something and holding onto hope.

Many people that have met life with immense amounts of success, failed countless times over before they reached their hopes and their dreams. People have drudged through the swamp waters of setbacks for years and sometimes even decades before they ever succeeded. These are the kind of people that didn't take no for answer and never gave up hoping, no matter what the situation was. If it was a dream that they held onto, the strong never allowed anything to get in the way, ever.

Whether it's Stephen King, Thomas Edison, or the countless other well-known individuals that come to mind, these people had to let go of their past disappointments and failures in order to continue to reach for their hopes and their dreams. Holding on to upsets and setbacks doesn't serve any individual who wants to achieve success at something in life; it holds you back. Do you think that Thomas Edison would have continued after 100 "failed" attempts to make the light bulb? Don't you think he got upset here and there when he suffered one setback after another? Of course he did. But not only did Edison fail 100 times, he failed over 10,000 times before he finally succeeded. When asked why he wasn't giving up by a newspaper reporter at the time, he simply remarked that he hadn't failed that many times, he was that many times closer to achieving his goal and figuring out what didn't work.

Of course this may sound like an extreme example to you, but the truth of the matter is that failure is a part of life. We all fail at some things some times, but it's important not to beat yourself up over it. Letting go of the past is hard, and that's the truth, especially if it's a past that you've held onto for a long time, but it's necessary to let go. The sooner that you realize that this behavior is not serving you, the sooner you can let go and move on with your life. If you're stuck in a situation where your past has dashed your hopes for the future, then you need to take severe action right now to make a change. You have to associate enough pain to not changing, that you have no choice but to change.

LEARNING FROM YOUR PAST

If you can take your past experiences, accept them, understand them, and learn from them, then you will be able to build a foundation for hope and prosperity in your future. You need to use your experiences as a platform for future growth, and not allow them to stifle you and hold you back. Too many times in our lives, we allow the pain and upset of past experiences to hold us back. Don't allow yourself to fall into this trap. Remind yourself that you are not your past and your experiences don't define you, they help to guide you. Whether you made some big mistakes, or small ones, use them to learn and grow, and move past the pain.

When Jonathan, the 47-year-old ex-homeless man, talked about his past, the audience could see the pain that he went through in the flashes of his eyes as he retold his story. However, Jonathan had come to accept his past, understand it and learned from it, and you could tell in his mannerisms and speech that he seemed like a stronger person through it all. Although he let his past define him at one point in his life, that trigger of the death of his friend allowed him to finally take a very good look at his life and his past behaviors of addiction, and learn from it in order to move on. He no longer made excuses for himself and felt sorry for himself. He picked himself up, and moved on.

Now, by no means is this easy to do. Yes, it's simple to talk about it and discuss the steps required in doing so, but actually sitting down to take a deep look at yourself and your behaviors takes a lot of work and a true sincerity and honesty that most people simply cannot do when it comes to analyzing their own behaviors. If this is the case for you then talk to friends and loved ones and try to get them to help you identify some of your behaviors and patterns that may be self-deprecating you. If you don't feel like you can talk to someone close to you, then seek professional guidance, but speaking out and opening up to people close to you will help you in the process of becoming a better person. There's no excuse for not pursuing a brighter, better future by understanding your past behaviors to learn from them, accept them, and move on.

6
LAYING THE GROUNDWORK FOR HOPE

"We must accept finite disappointment, but never lose infinite hope."
Martin Luther King Jr.

"I have a dream that one day this nation will rise up and live out the true meaning of its creed. 'We hold these truths to be self-evident that all men are created equal'.

"I have a dream that one day out on the red hills of Georgia the sons of former slaves and the sons of former slave owners will be able to sit down together at the table of brotherhood.

"I have a dream that one day even the state of Mississippi, a desert state sweltering with the heat and injustice of oppression, will be transformed into an oasis of freedom and justice.

"I have a dream that my four little children will one day live in a nation where they will not be judged by the color of their skin but by the content of their character.

"I have a dream today.

"I have a dream that one day the state of Alabama, whose governor's lips are presently dripping with the words of interposition and nullification, will be transformed into a situation where little black boys and black girls will be able to join hands with little white boys and white girls and walk together as sisters and brothers.

"I have a dream today.

"I have a dream that one day every valley shall be exalted, every hill and mountain shall be made low, the rough places will be made plains and the crooked places will be made straight and the glory of the Lord shall be revealed and all flesh shall see it together. "

*****

In a day and age when all rational thought and ideology went against him, Martin Luther King Jr. still had a dream. His dream was that all men would be treated equal, as it was decreed in the American Declaration of Independence. He wasn't going to allow his people to stand for racial inequality, and be kept in the shackles of poverty any longer. His hope and his dreams were that some day, no matter the color of a person's skin, we would all be looked at equally. It's hard to fathom living in a world so segregated by color, as it once was not too long ago.

But in a day and age when there was no personal experience for him to fall back on, Martin Luther King Jr. still had hope. He had hope that his children, and his children's children, and their children after that wouldn't suffer the same racial oppression any longer. He wanted a world where his children could roam free, work where they wanted, live where they wanted, travel how they wanted, and be free in an unsegregated society. He had no personal experiences to base his hope off of, but he did use history as his reference point. Martin Luther King Jr., a pastor, preached about love and non-violence, often quoting passages from the Bible. He used Jesus as his historical experience and looked to others like Gandhi, who had lead a peaceful protest of the people of India against the oppressive British rule that eventually helped win its country's freedom and independence.

When you look to the past, and people who have strived to achieve their dreams, it's not something that should impress you, but rather something that should impress upon you what's possible no matter what your situation is. Whatever it is that you hope for and strive for in your life, others that have come before you have achieved much of it. You can use the experience of others as further support to strengthen your own belief system to prop up your hope, your dreams, and your goals. No matter what it is, never allow yourself for a moment to think that you cannot achieve it simply because you feel like your situation is far different than others.

In order to begin laying the groundwork for more hope in your life, you must alter your beliefs and look at experiences in your life differently, or look to the experience of others. By doing this, you not only support your new beliefs in achieving your hopes and your dreams, but you unlock the power of the invisible forces of thoughts in your life. In 1909 Prentice Mulford wrote a book called "Thoughts are Things," where he chronicled how to use the power of thought to improve your present situation in life to manifest that which you desire. Of course, thought without action will not work, but the power of thought when combined with action and supported by the proper belief systems, can move mountains.

Today, the thought movement is still a very powerful

one, and it's important to note that in life, whatever it is that you focus on, will come to pass. If you focus on the negative, negative things will happen, but if you stay focused on the positive, positive things will happen. This does not mean that you should ignore situations that require your attention, but it does mean that if you allow yourself to drain all of your emotional and mental energy worrying about a certain situation, you will make it worse in your mind, and you will manifest physical affects of that worry.

To lead a life of hope, and to keep your dreams alive doesn't mean that you should be optimistic about everything that has happened to you in your past. If you've had bad things happen, use those as the platform of a costly but very educational experience in your life that you can now use to propel yourself into the future. Constantly focusing on the negative and living in the past will lead nowhere good for you. Learn to let go, and focus your thoughts on good things that will help you contribute and grow in life, and not on things that are self-defeating. Instead of hatred, harbor love; instead of resentment, harbor forgiveness.

If you are truly ready to begin laying the groundwork for a more hopeful life, then there are a few steps you should follow. Aside from having a clear understanding of what it is that you want to achieve from life by setting some well-defined goals, you should use the following six daily tips to help you foster more hope at any point in your life.

TIP 1 – BE KIND TO YOURSELF

Continually beating yourself up for past mistakes will never serve you well. You have to learn to let go of your past, and accept it as being part of your life. Use your past as a learning experience, and just because something bad happened to you in your life, it doesn't mean you need to hate yourself. Be kind to yourself; love yourself; forgive yourself. Allow yourself room to make mistakes because it's part of who we are and it's part of growing and maturing, so allow it to make you a better person. Don't allow things that have happened to you define you; you're not defined by your past.

When you begin to be kind to yourself and allow yourself some breathing room, a whole new world will open up to you. Each day when you awake, remind yourself of all the things that you're thankful for and be happy for all the good things in your life. No matter who you are, there are always those out there who are in a worse situation, so try to remind yourself of that and live in a state of gratitude. In North Korea, there are dozens of prison camps that enslave hundreds of thousands of its people to a life of servitude. They are left in famine like conditions, tortured, and worked to death. There is a lot to be thankful for in this world, so be kind to your self starting right now. Even if you don't have a penny to your name, and you are deeply in debt, be thankful for all that you have.

When we leave this life, money and material things won't be able to come with us. Whatever you do on this earth, do it to help and serve others, and make sure that you are always providing value and contributing as much as you can. When you begin to live with an attitude of gratitude and begin to be kind to yourself, the whole world will take on a new meaning to you. In this state, you can happily succeed instead of succeeding to be happy. We all need a little bit more gratitude in our lives. Don't wait, take out a pen and paper and right down all the things you're thankful for in your life, and be sincere. Start living each day with kindness, love and forgiveness in your heart and you'll be able to step away from the shackles of hate and anger that bind you in this world.

TIP 2 – CREATE EMPOWERING RITUALS

We all want something in life, no matter how big or small it may be; these are the things in life that we hope for. No matter what it is in life that you hope for or dream about, afford yourself some time in each day to simply take a break. If it's a sunny day outside, take a stroll somewhere and listen to the sights and sounds of life around you. Take a look at the children and see how excited they are about life and how thrilled they are to discover anything that they come upon. You used to be like this once too. Remember that, and hold onto that. Don't ever forget that life is a beautiful gift, and it should never be taken for granted.

When you create empowering rituals in your life

through the expansion of your gratitude and love, it will serve you as you strive to not only fulfill your hopes, but to fulfill them from a state of happiness. Examples of empowering rituals are spending the first 30 minutes of your day in exercise or in thought about all the things in life you love or are grateful for. An empowering ritual could be a simple 15-minute meditation exercise where you sit motionless, in a state of complete awareness of your physical body and the world around you.

Whatever ritual you create, find something empowering and make sure that you do it. Look beyond even your own personal needs and look to help others. Your empowering ritual may be to spend time once a week at a homeless shelter giving and supporting others suffering through hardships in life. Whatever it is, find something and do it; don't wait around for the perfect opportunity to come to you.

TIP 3 – REDUCE THE NOISE

Let's face it, there's a lot of noise in our lives today. From the moment you awake to the moment you go to sleep, you are bombarded with noise whether it's within your household or outside of it. From the morning news and talk shows, to attention requiring children, Internet and social media, and just about everything in between, noise is everywhere. But this high level of noise also causes a high amount of stress.

American mainstream media has a tendency to make the noise that it shares, negative noise. From violence across the world, to violence on the home front, media constantly portrays violence as a source of increasing their viewership. This is not to say that an overall understanding of the world and its problems is not a good thing, but an excessive amount of noise, especially noise that portrays negative situations, is not good for anyone.

Your job is to reduce the amount of noise in your life. Limit how much time you spend on social media, read a book instead of watching the news, or go for a jog and listen to soothing music. If you can put yourself into a more centered and happy state, you will be much more likely to pursue your hopes and your dreams without feeling so stressed out. There's nothing worse than working so hard that you feel you're going to burst if you work any harder. Put your mind at ease from time to time and try to reduce the amount of noise in your life; you'll be happy you did.

TIP 4 – DAILY AFFIRMATIONS

You may not think that affirmations have the power to change your life but they do. Affirmations can alter your train of thought and retrain your subconscious mind to think in a more positive and hopeful manner. Since human beings have more than 60,000 thoughts in any given day, most of which you are not aware of, ingraining positive thoughts and affirmations into your mind can change the course of your life.

If you've never done affirmations before, they are not too difficult. The first thing that you need to do is identify the negative scripts that you run in your head. For example, if you've been trying to lose weight, you need to first identify any negative thoughts you have associated to weight loss. Things like "Dieting is like going through hell," or "I'll never lose weight," or "How am I ever going to give up chocolate chip cookies?" You need to rewrite the scripts of your life when you do affirmations. Come up with something that affirms your hopes and your goals such as "Every day, in every way, I will get stronger, better and faster," or "This is no longer a diet, this is a way of life, and I choose to live healthy, eat clean foods, and exercise because it makes me look great, but more importantly, feel great."

Make sure that you write down the affirmations that you come up with for yourself. Don't just think about these in your mind. Actually write them down. If you want to make a change in your life, you have to take the time to do the work. Write down the affirmations, and ingrain them in your mind. Read them the moment you wake up until you memorize them all, and then repeat them day and night. If you find yourself wavering from your objective, repeat the affirmations again. Do this until it is a part of you; do it until it is ingrained in you.

If you have difficulty with your affirmations, place them somewhere that will make them always visible to you. If you work from home, place them next to your computer screen, or tape them to your wall, or to your refrigerator. Do anything that you need to do so that you can reaffirm, every single day, just what you want to believe in. Affirmations can be a powerful tool in helping change your outlook and beliefs, but they require a sincere desire to change. Try using emotionally charged language in your affirmations in order to make them stick.

TIP 5 – BREAK FROM THE NORM

Sometimes, you simply have to take a break from the norm in order to elevate your mood and keep your hopes and goals in front of you. If you always run along the same path, change it up; if you travel to work along the same route, take a different one. If you always eat the same thing for lunch, try something different. Although we are all creatures of habit, breaking your patterns sometimes can help interrupt not only your behavior, but also your train of thought. If you find yourself always craving a chocolate bar at 3pm, go for a walk at that time, or have a granola bar on hand instead. Do whatever you can in order to interrupt your patterns, especially if those patterns have not been serving you in the past.

Most of us can get very comfortable and deep-seated in

our patterns, especially when they are negative patterns. You have to do whatever you can to interrupt and break them, because if you can't do that then you run the risk of being a slave to those patterns for a very long time. Breaking your patterns can sound so simple and easy to do, but as you'll notice, your brain takes over and goes into autopilot mode when you are busy milling about your day. When you're sitting at home on the couch watching the television your autopilot behavioral patterns of going to the kitchen for some unhealthy snacks may take over. These types of patterns can be detrimental to you, and they can also be very difficult to break.

Awareness is the key to breaking your patterns. If you can be aware of your actions, and be honest with yourself that they are not serving you, and you'll be much further ahead in trying to break those patterns. By doing things that are not part of your daily routine, you can change it up so that you become more acute and aware throughout the day. This will help to serve you in breaking any of your patterns that may be negative because your brain won't be functioning on autopilot. When that happens, not only does your conscious mind take over, but also your subconscious thoughts and patterns stop repeating themselves when you become aware of them. When you interrupt these patterns, you break the negative behaviors and thought processes.

If you're attempting to make some changes in your life, and you're truly committed to changing, then breaking from the norm is a vital tool in the path to your success. This pattern interruption can help you realign your focus by being more aware of what it is that you constantly focus on throughout the course of the day. Pattern interruption should start from the moment that you wake up, to the moment that you go to bed. If your alarm usually goes off at 6:30am, set it to 6am and go for a run or a walk outside first instead. Whatever it takes, you have to interrupt your

HAVE A LITTLE HOPE

patterns and take a break from the norm. Pull yourself off of that couch and do something active, and change it up. You'll be glad you did.

TIP 6 – SHOW LOVE AND GRATITUDE

Human beings require love to survive; it is one of the basic human needs necessary in our lives to go on. Without love, we can wither away, but it's important to not only receive love, but to give it as well. When you give love you open yourself up to the world to also receive love in return. That love can come in so many different forms but in order to truly open yourself up to receive love, you must give it first. Life is truly a gift, and all too often we get so caught up in our daily routines that we forget about the things that matter the most. But when a tragedy strikes we are reminded of all the things that we love and that are important to us in this world. Why does it take tragedy to make us realize how important the love in our lives is?

By being grateful and expressing love, your life takes on

a new meaning and dimension. You go from a state of succeeding to be happy, to happily succeeding. But ask some of the most destitute people on the planet what it means to be happy, and they'll simply point to the ones around them, and smile warmly. In life, the people that are around us that love and support us matter the most. You can't take money and riches once you die, so unload your problems and try to show more love and gratitude in the world and you'll receive it back 10-fold.

7
LEARN TO DREAM BIG

"Every great dream begins with a dreamer. Always remember, you have within you the strength, the patience, and the passion to reach for the stars to change the world." – Harriet Tubman

Since the dawn of time, man has learned to dream big. As each dream came to fruition, beliefs would expand, visions would enlarge, and bigger dreams were dreamt. We've built buildings into the sky, created flying machines, sent men to the moon, and perfected global communications all because we've learned to dream big. But, the sad part of our epic history has been that large percentage of the world that doesn't dream big. Those people out there have trained themselves not to dream big because in their experience it just leads to disappointment and failure. This group of people have been so disappointed with what life has brought to pass that dreaming big itself has become a distant dream that they wouldn't dare try and conjure up.

HAVE A LITTLE HOPE

Human beings are meant to thrive, and not just survive. Of course, survival is our basic instinct, but when your survival needs have been meant, you have to dream big. You have to widen your vision of thought and imagine what life would be like if you could have the things that your heart desires the most. Don't be afraid to do this; don't be afraid to dream big. Don't be afraid of what others have to say, or how they may react when you start making strides towards your dreams, your hopes and your desires. Don't ever let anyone crush your sense of spirit and motivation, and come in the way between you and your dreams. Don't let people bring you down with their negative comments and actions. You're bigger than that and you're bigger than them.

It doesn't matter what you dream of, you can make it come to pass. Just imagine for a moment how far we've come in the world. How many people were told that they couldn't do something and they did? How many people told Helen Keller she couldn't achieve her dreams? How many people told Edison he would never invent the light bulb? How many people laughed and scoffed at Abraham Lincoln for dreaming that he would free the slaves in North America? How many people thought that winning their country's independence from any other suppressive power would be impossible, yet it was done? How many people told Gandhi or Martin Luther King Jr. that they would never achieve their dreams of freedom and liberation for their people?

People achieve their dreams all the time. Every single moment of every single day, someone is achieving his or her dreams. People who were told there was no possible way, no matter what they did or thought, have prevailed. From overcoming cancer, to beating poverty, to landing on the moon, and you name it, we have done it. You cannot allow the negativity that evades society to affect and alter your dreams. You have to believe in them so strongly, and harbor them so close to your heart, and push towards them with a burning desire unlike ever before, that the universe has no choice but to reward you with the accomplishment of those dreams.

Whatever your circumstances are today, it's only your current reality. No matter what you have presently in your life, from finances, to relationships, to health, all of that is only what exists right now. You are so much more than just that and there is so much more for you out there in the world. By dreaming big, you tap into what French Philosophers refer to as The Collective Conscious. This phenomenon, which has been documented throughout literature and history, provides an infinite amount of resources for anything you may conjure up. Whatever your dream is, don't be afraid to dream it and dream it big.

No matter whom you ask throughout history and time that has dreamt big dreams, they'll all tell you the same thing. These individuals had dreams that were so prevalent in their minds, so vividly imagined that, although they were unsure just how they were going to achieve those dreams, they knew they were going to achieve them. Their dreams were a must. Anytime something is a must in your life, all the impediments crumble away. There's nothing that will stand in the way between you and a dream that you hold that fervently in your heart. Nothing.

Never be afraid to ask the universe for what you want. Because, when you do this with a passion and burning desire from your heart, and you're able to vividly imagine it coming to pass, it will. You may not be sure today how it's going to get done, but you have to know that it is going to get done. It doesn't matter what it is. It doesn't matter how many people told you it couldn't be done. It doesn't matter at all. If you can imagine it, and you can dream it, then you can do it. As cheeky as this sounds it is completely true. But as soon as you begin to doubt, falter, and stray from your dreams, then your chances drop exponentially of achieving them. You must keep the momentum going, and you must not give up.

Don't ever give up. Don't ever let go of something you once held so deeply inside of you. And don't be afraid to ask the universe for just what it is that you want. No matter what it is that you want in your life, you can have it, if you can just learn to ask for it in the right way. You have to put the passion and emotional meaning behind why it is you want what you want in life. It doesn't matter how big it is, if you can ask for it and dream it then you can have it. It's similar to driving a car in the dead of the night, you can only see a hundred or so feet in front of you on a long distance trip, but as long as you keep traveling in the right direction, you will reach your destination. Your hopes and your dreams are no different. People who were once laughed at or scoffed at people for dreaming big, those same people made those dreams a reality and you certainly can too.

There's nothing that separates you from someone else that has achieved their dreams other than the burning desire to reach for the stars even if you fall flat on your face many times over. The most successful people in the world have failed time and time again, but it was through those failures that they were able to find the errs in their ways, make adjustments, and refocus their efforts to achieving their hopes and their dreams. The big difference is that many people will give up before they reach their goals; many people will call it quits just before they're about to succeed. Many people will just give up.

While success in anything that you want is either through inspiration or desperation, no success is possible without dreaming first. Don't be afraid to dream, and don't be afraid to dream big. But don't just be and expect things to fall into your lap, put some motion behind the emotion. By combining massive action with your dreams, and doing a little bit each and every day as you strive towards your goals, you will fulfill your hopes and your dreams. It's only a matter of time.

Don't ever give up because someone tells you that it can't be done. Don't ever be willing to sacrifice what you want in exchange for a life that's full of hopelessness and despair. Don't ever be afraid to dream because one day, you will make that dream come true. <u>You know you will.</u>

THANK YOU

If you enjoyed the book, I would really appreciate it if you could take a few moments and share your thoughts by posting a review on Amazon. If this book inspired you in any way shape or form, I would love to hear about it in a book review.

I hope that my care and sincerity come across in my writing because in the end I write to bring value to other people's lives. I hope that this book has brought some value to your life. I truly do.

Here is the link that you can use to post a review on Amazon for this book - http://www.amazon.com/dp/B00CGZCFZU

I wish you all the best in the pursuit of your hopes and dreams. Never give up hope. Never.

-RL

Printed in Great Britain
by Amazon.co.uk, Ltd.,
Marston Gate.